Giuseppe Marasco - Mrwatch93

MICROBRANDS BOOK III

Inside microbrands and independent watchmakers

GENÈVE 2024

Title | Microbrands Book III Genève Edition 2024 Insid
Microbrands and Independent Watchmakers
Author | Mrwatch93
ISBN | 979-12-22730-41-7

You can print
Via Marco Biagi 6, 73100 Lecce
www.youcanprint.it
Made by humans

To my family.

INTRODUCTION

Hello and welcome to the Microbrands book 2024 Genève special edition!

Cannot believe we are here with a third edition and I am very happy because this is not the classic edition I publish every year but this one is distributed at Time to Watches event in Geneva in this 2024 so it's a very special book for me.

Distributing this book for the first time in Geneva represents a great achievement for me because as many watch enthusiasts know, Geneva is an important watchmaking hotspot where various events such as Watches and Wonders, Time to Watches or Geneva Watch Days take place every year.

Depending on the event, you can find big brands, independent brands or smaller brands. Bringing my book to one of these events was therefore a little dream come true and I would like to thank my readers who buy my books every year and at every release.

This edition is basically a preview of the 2024 edition of the Microbrands Book Inside microbrands and independent watchmakers series that will be released in the coming months and features a special cover and pages dedicated to Time to Watches.

In this edition you will find not only microbrands but also amazing independents that are very close to *haute horologerie* and also some interesting new brands/ watchmakers I really hope you don't already know!

Have a nice reading!

TIME TO WATCHES
EXHIBITION | EXPERIENCE | EVENTS
10 - 14 APRIL 2024
HEAD — Genève
timetowatches.com
In partnership with
—HEAD
Genève

Time to Watches
The Inclusive Watch Event in Geneva

As MrWatch93 wrote the pages of his first book, someone else felt a lack of communication in watchmaking world. A story that put small watchmakers in the background in favor of the giants of the sector. Christian Wipfli, a passionate watch enthusiast, translated the need of giving voice to independents and micro-brands in an event held every year in Geneva: Time to Watches.

Its first edition (2022) had great success despite the aftermath of the pandemic. In 2024 TW third edition is taking place from Wednesday 10 April to Sunday 14 April.

In the cradle of Swiss watchmaking, alongside the most elite *maisons*, this event is developed by focusing on inclusivity. There are no barriers or preconceptions other than those of quality. Every new concept or innoative idea are welcome, no matter your type of movement, your target or your prices. The atmosphere during Time to Watches is created to make everyone feel comfortable. During the event there is the possibility to interacts with the brands and try their watches all day long!

ANDERSEN Genève

When it comes to independent watchmaking ANDERSEN Genève has been among the most exclusive brands for many years.

The founder Svend was born in Denmark in 1942 and after his diploma from the Danish Watchmaker School integrated in the Royal Technological Institute of Copenhagen, he went to Switzerland in 1963 in order to see how the world's best watches were made. In 1969 he put a clock into a bottle and was then called the "watchmaker of the impossible". Patek Philippe got interested in ANDERSEN's creation and, in 1969, Svend ANDERSEN joined their "Atelier des grandes complications". Svend ANDERSEN launched his own workshop in the late 70's after having spent 9 years at Patek Philippe.

He started his career as independent watchmaker by first manufacturing cases and making pocket watches for Italian collectors. ANDERSEN Genève is well known for developing complicated watches like worldtime watches, Jumping Hours , annual calendar, perpetuel calendar, and even secular perpetual calendar (programmed for 400 years!). The 38mm Jumping hour is one of the most famous and fascinating latest creation and is limited to 50 peices.

Founder
Svend Andersen
•
Owner
Pierre-Alexandre Aeschlimann
•
Founding year
1980
•
Country
Switzerland
•
Type
Dress watch
•
Movement
Automatic
•
Price range
50k-150k CHF (~51k-155k €)
•
Collections
5
•
Website
andersen-geneve.ch

Jumping Hours

MOVEMENT	· Automatic Frédéric Piguet 11.50 with "Jumping Hours" by ANDERSEN Genève · 60H power reserve
CASE/DIAL	· Ø 38 mm · Brushed/polished platinum (Pt 950) case with welded lugs · 18ct pink gold hand guilloché "magical losanges" motive · Hours displayed at 12 o'clock, minutes at 6 · Open caseback
WATER RESISTANCE	30 m/3 atm
CRYSTAL	Sapphire crystal front and back with double sided anti-reflect coating
LUME	No
STRAP	Nubuck strap
PRICE	48800 CHF (~50500 €)

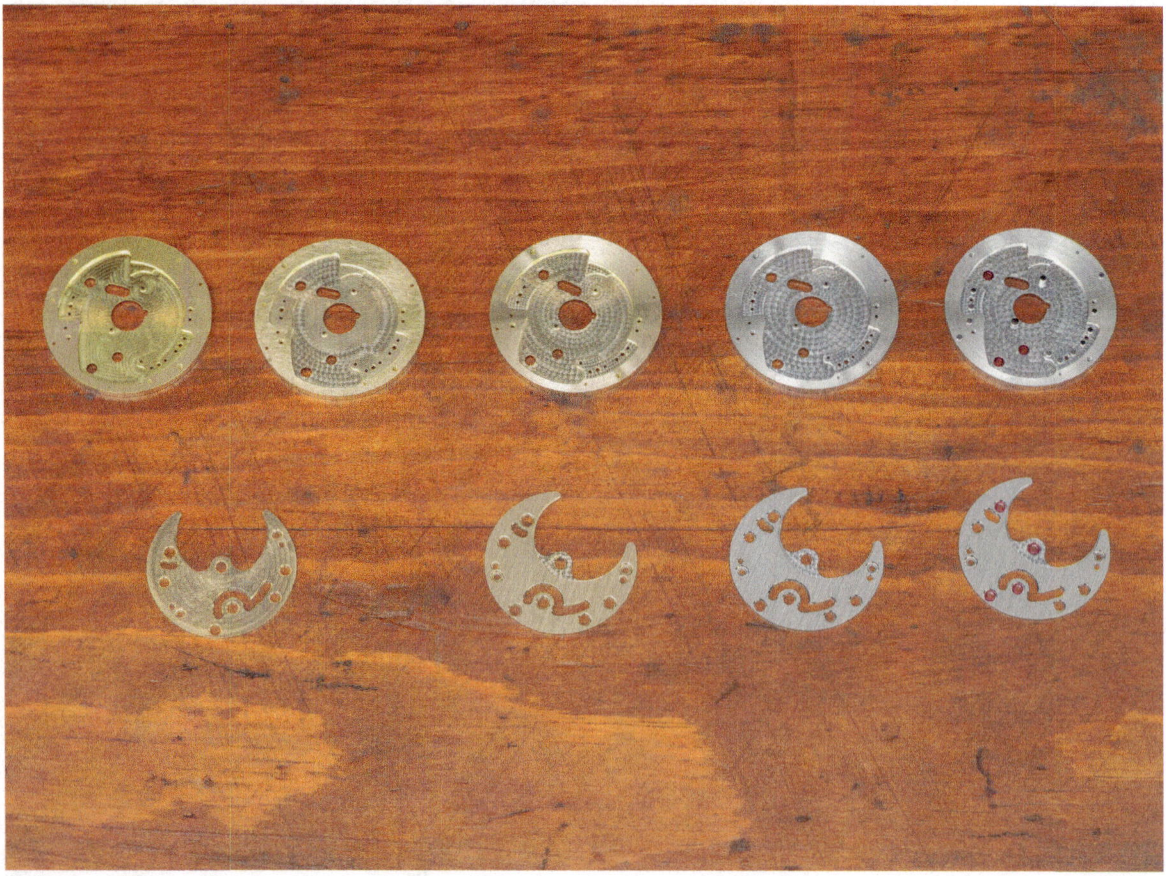

WHY BUY?

ANDERSEN Genève is certainly not an affordable brand precisely because we are talking about haute horlogerie.

Considering the materials, complications and limited editions, the watches and finishes offered by this independent brand are of far greater value than many Swiss brands which, on the other hand, offer less complicated timepieces with even less important materials at the same price.

The dials are small works of art that can be appreciated with macro shots and are certainly a spectacle for the eyes, especially when viewed with a magnifying glass.

APIAR
Additive
AUTOMATIC

APIAR

Behind each brand there are people who are trying in their own way to revolutionise watchmaking by using new techniques and technologies. This is exactly what Apiar is doing, revolutionising watchmaking "one layer at a time" as they said. Indeed the most interesting part of this brand are their unique watch cases manufactured through a laser powder bed fusion process. This cutting-edge technology is mainly found within the aerospace industry and high-end automotive applications. The process involves fine grade 23 titanium powder particles selectively melted into fine 0.06mm layers. Over thousands of layers, the near net shape cases are then printed and ready for post processing and polishing. This additive manufacturing process allows design liberties which are not possible with conventional subtractive watch manufacturing processes and also it gives the possibility to have most of the timepieces made in the UK. This not only significantly minimizes waste compared to traditional methods, but it also effectively diminishes carbon emissions linked to the global transportation of parts by primarily relying on a UK-based supply chain. The results of this process are algorithmically skeletonised cases filled with complex lattice geometries never seen before in the watch industry.

FOUNDER
Matt and Sam

•

FOUNDING YEAR
2022

•

COUNTRY
UK

•

TYPE
3D Printed

•

MOVEMENT
Automatic

•

PRICE RANGE
2160£
(2517€)

•

COLLECTIONS
1

•

WEBSITE
apiar.co.uk

INVENIRE

MOVEMENT	· La Joux-Perret G100 version soignée vis bleues · 68h power reserve
CASE/DIAL	· Ø 39 mm · Skeletonised case with latticed interior · 5 hand painted matte colours available: black, onyx grey, engineering orange, oxford blue and racing green · Made in UK.
WATER RESISTANCE	100 m/10 atm
CRYSTAL	Sapphire crystal with AR coating
LUME	Hands, indices
STRAP	Hand craft leather
PRICE	2160£ (2517€)

WHY BUY?

These watches are the result of significant hi-tech skills applied in the watch industry and considering the technology used for these timepieces I personally find the price to be very honest. Just think how big the price could be if a big brand starts creating something like this.

Most parts of the watch are made in the UK except for the movements (Swiss-made), the crystals (Germany) and the hands (France). The guilloche pattern dial and the case are a a feast for the eyes.

ARCTURUS

ARCTURUS

Arcturus Watches was founded by Alexander Ian Loh whilst he was reading law in university in the UK. He was fascinated by the oscillating balance wheel of a ETA 6497 movement and began taking watches apart and building his own timepieces with parts that he could source online.

Eventually, he took the leap to try his hand at designing a piece that he could truly call his own, starting with sketches on law tutorial papers in his small Elmfield House student apartment. Alexander's designs pay homage to his home, Singapore, drawing inspiration from the rich and abundant architecture and nature that surrounds him in Singapore (also proudly known as the Lion City and the Garden City) and this is evident in the timepieces produced by Arcturus which incorporate elements of Singapore in it's designs. The core principle of Arcturus is that of "No Compromise" and this shows in the design language and finishing of the timepieces produced by Arcturus.

Arcturus inaugural launch, the LION CITY 1, was sold out worldwide and is still highly sort after by collectors till today, and serves as a testament to the effort Arcturus puts in every watch they launch.

FOUNDER
Alexander Iian Loh

FOUNDING YEAR
2017

COUNTRY
Singapore

TYPE
Dress watch

MOVEMENT
Hand wound

PRICE RANGE
800-1420US
(700-1300€)

COLLECTIONS
2

WEBSITE
arcturuswatches.sg

Lion City 2

MOVEMENT	·Peacock SL-5200 Flying Tourbillon ·48H power reserve
CASE/DIAL	·Ø 44 mm ·White guilloche pattern ·Engraved and open caseback ·High polished, circular brush, straight brush, sunburst brush
WATER RESISTANCE	50 m/5 atm
CRYSTAL	Sapphire crystal both front and back
LUME	No
STRAP	Leather strap
PRICE	968-1420 US$ (~900-1320 €)

Why buy?

Creating a new microbrand is not easy but creating a new microbrand with a tourbillon movement and making it affordable it is even more complicated.

Despite the very big dimensions of the watch and the affordable price (very affordable considering the movement) this timepiece doesn't look affordable and is carachterized by a very nice design and good choices like for example the caseback or the options of the dials.

ATELIER HOLGUR
FROMAND
ATELIER
HOLGUR

Atelier Holgur

Atelier Holgur is an independent watchmaker born out of a desire to build watches that could stand up to the rigours of life and adventure, incorporating high-end materials and techniques to deliver a uniquely rugged yet luxurious experience.

The brand was founded by two childhood friends, Asbjørn Simonen-Andersen and Matthew de Bakker, harnessing Matt's passion for design and horology, as well as Asbjørn's watchmaking heritage.
He grew up around his grandfathers' tools, and actually the Atelier Holgur name pays homage to him. Despite this affectionate look at the past, the brand aims to produce distinctive watches suited to the present day and beyond.

To emphasize its strong bond with current and future times, Atelier Holgur is determined to carve out a niche in the independent watch market, while supporting ocean conservation efforts around the world. As a passionate diver, Matt knows both colourful sub-aquatic wonders, as well as the damage and pollution that continues to erode our ocean. Atelier Holgur cares passionately about their products in terms of design, quality and performance. However, they equally care about the impact of each actions on the planet, so they chose to play an active role in doing good through their business.

FOUNDER
Asbjørn Simonen-Andersen & Matthew de Bakker

FOUNDING YEAR
2021

COUNTRY
Denmark - Singapore

TYPE
Diver

MOVEMENT
Automatic

PRICE RANGE
9850 CHF-11500 CHF

COLLECTIONS
1

WEBSITE
atelier-holgur.com

THE FRØMAND - EDITION FUMÈE

MOVEMENT	· Automatic Schwarz-Etienne ASE200 for Atelier Holgur · 86H power reserve
CASE/DIAL	· Ø 40 mm · Grade 5 titanium case with polished and microblasted finish · Open caseback · Sunburst Fumée Dial
WATER RESISTANCE	300 m/30 atm
CRYSTAL	Sapphire crystal front and back
LUME	Bezel, Hands, indexes
STRAP	· Two straps included made with recycled ocean plastic · Quick release
PRICE	11500 CHF (~12000 €)

Why buy?

The Frømand is a non-trivial innovative diver watch with features that rightfully place it in the "haute horlogerie" production.

The design of the dial is modern and minimal. This elegant simplicity hides a surprising open caseback that proudly shows a skeletonized movement with micro-rotor that is a jewel itself.

The materials have great value, specifically titanium, which lends lightness and charm.

In my opinion, these characteristics coupled with a workmanlike realisation of components and assembly justify the entry-level luxury pricing. Added to this is the commitment to safeguarding the oceans for which they are selecting the best partners to fund initiatives to help protect the underwater ecosystem. Part of the waste recovered from the oceans is directly used by Atelier Holgur to produce their straps.

BAUCHE
BAUCHE

BAUCHE WATCHES

Ranndie is an experienced Marketing and Communications professional with a decade of experience in luxury hospitality. A watch enthusiast by heart, his designs, concepts and storytelling are heavily influenced by independent luxury brands, avant-garde & concept timepieces, and literary expressions of everyday objects.

Derived from the horological term *ebauche*, Bauche represents the physical manifestation of a horological timepiece conceived in the vision of telling a story through time. Every creation begins life on a blank canvas, where art and storytelling takes centre stage.

Inspired by the hallmarks of everyday objects and professions, each design explores different cultures, themes and literary expressions, while reimagining third party movements with a creative twist. Striking a balance between artistic creativity and the classical aesthetics of horology, each creation becomes a compelling conversation starter to every collector's distinguished watch collection.

FOUNDER
Ranndie Seah
•
FOUNDING YEAR
2021
•
COUNTRY
Singapore
•
TYPE
Art Piece Dress watch
•
MOVEMENT
Automatic
•
PRICE RANGE
855-1088 US$
•
COLLECTIONS
2
•
WEBSITE
www.bauche.watch

STARGAZER CARINA NEBULA

MOVEMENT	· Miyota9133Automatic · 40H power reserve
CASE/DIAL	· Ø 41 mm · 904L stainless steel case · 3 layer stacked dial: Coloured MoP or Abalone MoP; IP treated meteorite stone; IP treated stamped guilloche
WATER RESISTANCE	120 m/12 atm
CRYSTAL	Sapphire crystal with AR Coating
LUME	Hands and indexes
STRAP	Black leather strap
PRICE	888-1088 US$ (~920-1000 €)

Why buy?

The Stargazer Carina Nebula series is a captivating fusion of traditional and modern watch-making inspired by the James Webb Space Telescope's mesmerizing images of the Carina Nebula. With six evocative timepieces driven by re-imagining the Miyota 9133 movement with a creative twist, each dial combines the luminescent Mother of Pearl stones, IP Plated Meteorite Stone and IP Plated Guilloche dials, that conceptualises the captivating aesthetic and the visually compelling Carina Nebula.

The 904L offers strength and lightness and provides visual interest and weight with its four-cornered facets on the bezel.

The case leans towards a two-tone dressy polished surface - brushed and mirrored polishing on the case topsides and bezel, carefully ensuring that the star of the show remains in focus without forcefully pulling the eye away from the allure of its visually compelling space-like aesthetic.

BEHREN
INVENTOR

BEHRENS

Behrens is well known for its unique, modern and complex design models and focus on the reimagination of the future watchmaking with boundless creativity. This brand plays a lot with the space and immainagination.

There are many timepieces and collections available, allowing people with very different tastes to find their ideal watch. Although the models produced are not characterised by very high prices, the research, quality and uniqueness of each collection is evident. For example the models B018 based on an imagination of the Mothership that the alien would use for traveling to Earth or the B027 characterised by a Chain drive system or the BHR030 "Ultra light" based on an ancient Chinese historical tool called "Hu", especially used as narrow tablets for recording notes and orders. Every watch made takes inspiration from the present, the past and even the imagination of a future watchmaking.

FOUNDER
Lin Bingqiang

FOUNDING YEAR
2012

COUNTRY
China

TYPE
Unique design

MOVEMENT
Automatic, hand-wound

PRICE RANGE
1350-13500 US$
(~ 1230-13820 €)

COLLECTIONS
5+

WEBSITE
behrens2012.com

B027

MOVEMENT	·Hand-wound caliber BM01 ·45H power reserve
CASE/DIAL	·Ø 43 mm ·Grade 5 Titanium case with black coating ·Chain drive system ·Black texured dial that simulate the Moon surface ·Open caseback
WATER RESISTANCE	50 m/5 atm
CRYSTAL	Sapphire crystal both front and back
LUME	Indexes
STRAP	Leather strap
PRICE	Sold out

B018

MOVEMENT	· Automatic SWB18-200 ·38H power reserve
CASE/DIAL	·Ø 44 mm ·316L stainless steel case with up to 40 facets ·Twin rollers time display system ·Sapphire crystal dial Engraved caseback
WATER RESISTANCE	30 m/3 atm
CRYSTAL	Sapphire crystal
LUME	Indexes
STRAP	·Rubber strap ·Quick release
PRICE	3600US$ (~3300 €)

BHR030

MOVEMENT	· Hand-wound cal. BM02 · 38H power reserve · Bi- retrograde (hours/ minutes)
CASE/DIAL	· Ø 42 mm · Grade 5 Titanium or carbon · Trapezoidal shape · 20 grams weight (titanium) head unit without strap
WATER RESISTANCE	300 m/30 atm
CRYSTAL	Sapphire crystal
LUME	No
STRAP	Fluoroelastomer with pin buckle.
PRICE	7600 US$ (~ 6900 €)

Why buy?

Each model made by this brand represents a step towards the future of watchmaking. Using state-of-the-art materials, unique movements and, above all, affordable prices, even for a young audience, allows one to truly appreciate the qualities Behrens has to offer and to bring in new enthusiasts.

Since these watches are unique and special, it is advisable to look for this brand at the many watchmaking events and try out the watches in order to choose the one that is right for you.

BERNEY

Based in L'Abbaye, in the heart of Switzerland's Vallée de Joux, the Berney brand has been offering traditional, refined and elegant watchmaking since 1972.

It all began when Henri Berney, a watchmaker by profession and founder of Berney Watch, decided to produce handcrafted wristwatches, watch pendants and rings watches made exclusively from Swiss components. Now in his nineties, Henri Berney continues to live from and for his passion of watchmaking. He still works daily to perpetuate this adventure, now accompanied by Carole, his granddaughter, who manages the company with enthusiasm, under the critical and knowing eye of her grandfather. Over the years, Berney has lost none of its DNA, and its watchmaking tradition and passion are reflected in a range of handcrafted and hand-decorated chronograph watches powered by new old stock Valjoux movements. The most original collection is certainly that of jewelry: the time leaves the wrist to be found around the neck on a pendant and even on the finger with a ring that acts as a watch. Berney's vision is to maintain the brand's emblematic pieces and give a second life to a watch or component by extending the product life cycle as much as possible.

FOUNDER
Henri Berney
•
FOUNDING YEAR
1972
•
COUNTRY
Switzerland
•
TYPE
Dress watch
•
MOVEMENT
Hand wound
•
PRICE RANGE
3000-18000 €
•
COLLECTIONS
+5
•
WEBSITE
berneywatch.ch

Berney VJ88 G

MOVEMENT	·Hand-wound Valjoux 13”88 dating 1960’s ·Chronograph ·Moon phase ·38H power reserve
CASE/DIAL	·Ø 39 mm ·Polished 18 karat rose gold case ·Real mother-of-pearl dial with gold appliques ·Open caseback
WATER RESISTANCE	30 m/3 atm
CRYSTAL	Sapphire crystal both front and back
LUME	No
STRAP	Leather strap
PRICE	18000 CHF (~19145 €)

Berney VJ23 SQ

MOVEMENT	·Hand-wound Valjoux 13”23 dating 1950’s ·Chronograph ·38H power reserve
CASE/DIAL	·Ø 39 mm ·Polished 18 karat rose gold case ·Hand engraved skeleton dial ·Open caseback
WATER RESISTANCE	30 m/3 atm
CRYSTAL	Sapphire crystal both front and back
LUME	Hands
STRAP	Leather strap
PRICE	16000 CHF (~17017 €)

WHY BUY?

This is for me the first time I write about an independent watchmaker which creates also watch pendants and rings watches made exclusively from Swiss components. The beauty of the timepices and the finishes of these watches are unbelievable, specially for the skeleton model and the mother of pearl dial.

This brand needs more voice and more attention. Just pay attention always to duties as all these watches are shipped from Switzerland.

BILIĆ
BILIĆ

BILIC

Whenever a new watch brand is launched there are always many unknowns and it is important to bring something that is different but also original. Ante decided to go down this route by bringing something new and modern with some very special features.

Its first LEKLU collection features a smoked anthracite dial and a super-thin case measuring only 8.9 mm, making it not only very thin but also very light on the wrist. The first impression given by this watch is that it is a render whereas in reality it is only the effect given by the shading of the dial. The depth is certainly given by the angles of the case together with the right mix of polished and brushed finishes but above all by the dial characterised by 3 grooves also creating a play of shadows and light. The applied indexes are entirely covered with luminescent paste, making them very easy to read.

FOUNDER
Ante Bilic

FOUNDING YEAR
2023

COUNTRY
Australia

TYPE
Dress watch

MOVEMENT
Automatic

PRICE RANGE
550 €

COLLECTIONS
1

WEBSITE
bilicwatchco.com

LEKLU

MOVEMENT	• Automatic Sellita SW300 • 56H power reserve
CASE/DIAL	• Ø 40 mm • 316L stainless steel case • Smoked fume anthracite dial
WATER RESISTANCE	120 m/12 atm
CRYSTAL	Sapphire crystal
LUME	Hands and indexes
STRAP	Cumstom FKM rubber strap
PRICE	550 €

WHY BUY?

The first watch is always very difficult but this first model from Bilic has something special and makes it original and different from the usual 'first watch' we are used to. The dial and the super-slim case are a very strong point as is the price. The excellent use of the polished and satin finishes and the render effect given by the dial make this watch a successful project. Curious to know the future models of this brand and whether it will have good continuity.

BND Watches

BND Watches is a young French watchmaking house, created in 2021, by Vincent Bonnaud.

The philosophy of its brand can be summed up in these terms: "Back to the Past". Indeed, the brand's creator sees his neo-vintage watches as a time machine. The time mentioned here begins in the 1950s and ends in the 1980s. Why this period? The answer is simple: It was the time of iconic actors, great racing drivers and mythical motorcycle riders, but also legendary explorers. All these men have marked history and they have done it with their watches.

The creator of the brand pays homage to them with vintage inspired and robust dive watches. These timepieces are characterized by a great balance for price, finishes and quality and despite the brand's recent birth and especially after the pandemic, it has enjoyed great success. These timepieces are also worn by important collectors and personalities from the watch world.

FOUNDER
Vincent Bonnaud
•
FOUNDING YEAR
2021
•
COUNTRY
France
•
TYPE
Diver watch
•
MOVEMENT
Automatic
•
PRICE RANGE
455 €
•
COLLECTIONS
3
•
WEBSITE
bnd-watches.com

MNBLU

MOVEMENT	· Automatic NH35A · 41H power reserve
CASE/DIAL	· Ø 39.5 mm · 316L stainless steel case · Blue dial · Brushed finishing Unidirectional rotating bezel
WATER RESISTANCE	200 m/20 atm
CRYSTAL	Sapphire crystal
LUME	Hands, indexes, bezel
STRAP	Nylon strap
PRICE	455 €

MNBRO

MOVEMENT	· Automatic NH35A · 41H power reserve
CASE/DIAL	· Ø 39.5 mm · 316L stainless steel case · Brown dial · Brushed finishing Unidirectional rotating bezel
WATER RESISTANCE	200 m/20 atm
CRYSTAL	Sapphire crystal
LUME	Hands, indexes, bezel
STRAP	Nylon strap
PRICE	455 €

MNBLA

MOVEMENT	· Automatic NH35A · 41H power reserve
CASE/DIAL	· Ø 39.5 mm · 316L stainless steel case · Black dial · Brushed finishing Unidirectional rotating bezel
WATER RESISTANCE	200 m/20 atm
CRYSTAL	Sapphire crystal
LUME	Hands, indexes, bezel
STRAP	Nylon strap
PRICE	455 €

Why buy?

These watches are real tool-watches, robust, vintage as can be, very easy to wear and with exemplary finishes and perfect dimensions for going on an adventure.

If you want a good-looking dive watch for not a lot of money, this watch could be a great choice for sure.

CANOPY
WAKE ONE
20 ATM
CANOPY
WAKE ONE
20 ATM

Canopy Watch Co.

The first timepice realized by a microbrand is always difficult as it allows you to immediately understand the path you want to take. Sometimes very ambitious or perhaps too ambitious, while at other times perhaps too unambitious. Often many brands come out on the market with a watch too expensive or with features that do not satisfy collectors.

In this case Canopy's Wake One represents the starting point for the founders Machlen Polfliet and Ross Tomson: a 39 mm diver with Swiss movement and available in the classic steel version (Silver edition) or DLC coated (Midnight edition).

From this first model we already understand the use of particular materials will accompany Canopy throughout their path. In this diver we can see immediately carbon fiber on both the bezel and the crown. The presence of plenty of luminescence and the adjustable clasp along with the size of 39 mm case make us understand undoubtedly that this diver has its own character and that must be worn by everyone. Every timepiece is numbered and produced in a limited edition, making each watch unique and certainly even more appreciated by collectors.

FOUNDER
Machlen Polfliet & Ross Tomson

FOUNDING YEAR
2020

COUNTRY
USA

TYPE
Diver

MOVEMENT
Automatic

PRICE RANGE
599 US$ (~570 €)

COLLECTIONS
1

WEBSITE
canopywatchco.com

WAKE ONE

MOVEMENT	• Swiss automatic Sellita SW200-1 • 41H power reserve
CASE/DIAL	• Ø 39 mm • 316L stainless steel case (DLC coating available) • Forged carbon fiber bezel and crown insert • Display caseback
WATER RESISTANCE	200 m/20 atm
CRYSTAL	Sapphire crystal both front and back
LUME	Hands, indexes, bezel
STRAP	Stainless steel bracelet
PRICE	599 US$ (~570 €)

Why buy?

We know that the world of microbrands is very competitive and also surprising collectors with an innovative product is increasingly difficult. Despite this, Canopy has managed to create a watch with classic shapes but characterized by innovative elements and with a wise use of carbon fiber present both in the bezel and in the crown and also the lumen present on the bezel.

Key points of the watch are surely the dimensions of 39 mm, the price and the DLC variant for those who want a watch with a more aggressive look. Great packaging is a plus.

SWISS MADE

Done Watches

Done watches is an example of how micro-brands can also be synonymous with excellence. This brand realizes swiss made watches with high quality materials and interesting design. The mission of this brand is very clear, namely to make luxury watchmaking accessible to all.

Unfortunally, the world of watchmaking is often reserved for only a few people or high net worth individuals. Done, on the other hand, wants to give everyone the opportunity to have a top-of-the-range watch at a competitive price.

The founder Thierry was working for major watch brands when he daily noticed the staggering difference between the manufacturing price of a watch and its real price on the market. Everything started to create a luxury watch accesible to all watch lovers.

The name DONE (Done In Neuchâtel) denotes how this brand is linked to Swiss tradition.

Done's flagship model is the Mechanica, available in a classic or skeleton version, in a 35 mm ladies' version or for larger wrists with a 40 mm and 44 mm diameter.

FOUNDER
Thierry Clottu

FOUNDING YEAR
2016

COUNTRY
Switzerland

TYPE
Timeless Design

MOVEMENT
Manual & Automatic

PRICE RANGE
900-2200 €

COLLECTIONS
5

WEBSITE
donewatches.ch

Mechanica F01

MOVEMENT	· Automatic Skeleton STP 6-21 · 38H power reserve
CASE/DIAL	· Ø 40 mm · 316L Stainless steel case · Open caseback · Sapphire dial
WATER RESISTANCE	100 m/10 atm
CRYSTAL	Sapphire crystal
LUME	Hands and indexes
STRAP	Leather strap or stainless steel bracelet
PRICE	1615 €

WHY BUY?

Value for money is definitely the key point of this brand. Today's enthusiasts are very much influenced by this aspect and offering something of high quality at an affordable price is very important.

The Mechanica skeleton model is definitely the most interesting from Done watches, considering how expensive could be something like this especially from a Swiss brand. The packaging is also great for travellers consisting of a little leather travel case with two additional extra slots for carrying extra bracelets.

DWISS
SWISS
MADE

Dwiss Watches

Telling time in a different way. This is the motto of Dwiss, a Swiss brand founded by Rafael, desiner with a portfolio of hundreds of watches designed for more than 15 different brands and winner of important international design awards, like the Red Dot Design Award and the IF design award. Rafael is also former watch design teacher in Milan, Italy.

After understanding the founder's background, it is clear where the complexity of the design that characterises these watches comes from and which also makes them unique and special in reading the hours. There are many watches in the DWISS catalog but the M3S is one of the most interesting thanks also to the DWISS's signature hours. Representing a mysterious time display that utilizes a rotating disc beneath a multi-layered dial. Hours are elegantly presented within windows positioned between the indexes, with minutes and seconds displayed at the center. This brand is also working on increasingly high-end projects such as the tourbillon model RS1.

FOUNDER
Rafael Simoes Miranda

FOUNDING YEAR
2011

COUNTRY
Switzerland

TYPE
Design watch

MOVEMENT
Automatic

PRICE RANGE
1000-14000 US$
(~900-12800 €)

COLLECTIONS
5+

WEBSITE
dwiss.com

M3S

MOVEMENT	·Automatic Swiss Sellita SW200-1 ·42H power reserve
CASE/DIAL	·Ø 42 mm ·316L stainless steel case ·Shockproof protection Incabloc® ·Open dial & caseback
WATER RESISTANCE	200 m/20 atm
CRYSTAL	Sapphire crystal both front and back
LUME	No
STRAP	·Stainless steel bracelet ·Quick release
PRICE	1590 US$ (~1442 €)

RS1 - Tourbillon

MOVEMENT	·Concepto 8950 Tourbillon ·60H power reserve
CASE/DIAL	·Ø 45 mm ·316 L stainless steel ·IP Black case ·7-part multilayer structure ·Open caseback
WATER RESISTANCE	100 m/10 atm
CRYSTAL	Sapphire crystal both front and back
LUME	No
STRAP	Leather and canvas
PRICE	14000 US$ (~12806 €)

WHY BUY?

Success in the watchmaking world is always determined to a large extent by design. If the design is appreciated and loved by the public, then the brand is ready to grow and create new models.

Dwiss watches are very interesting and unique, especially the reading of the hours, which at first glance may not be immediately understood by other observers. The watch owner is then enticed to explain the hour reading, creating a unique feeling with their timepiece. The prices are honest and the size are weareble for most of the wrists thanks to the dimensions of 40-42 mm of mosts of the models except for the 45 mm tourbillon and R1.

EMBER
ROCKET
AUTOMATIC

EMBER

Ember Watch Company originated as a side project in 2020. Having worked in the bespoke furniture industry for over 15 years - undertaking roles in design, drawing, and project management - the founder John sought an opportunity to establish something unique, a venture that would not only unleash his creativity but also enable him to manage his own business. John has always had an interest in watches, though not to an obsessive degree. It struck him one day, to combine this hobby with his entrepreneurial ambitions. Following the inception of that initial idea, he immersed himself into the world of watches, delving into watch collecting and design.The design ethos of Ember Watch Company is to create stylish, modern watches with unique and original design language. The first model, 'Rocket', features an unusual case design, the most noticeable feature is the large facets that form the lugs. A bead-blasted finish creates a modern look, with the polished surface of the bezel catching the light and adding an element of interest. The colourful dials are a sandwich construction, with cutouts that don't indicate the hour positions, but instead fill the gaps between them. The negative space created indicates the hours. The bottom layer of the sandwich dial is lumed with BGW9 Superluminova, also used in the hour and minute hands.

FOUNDER
John Glinister
•
FOUNDING YEAR
2024
•
COUNTRY
UK
•
TYPE
Dress watch
•
MOVEMENT
Automatic
•
PRICE RANGE
£395(~458 €)
•
COLLECTIONS
1
•
WEBSITE
emberwatchcompany.com

Rocket

MOVEMENT	·Automatic NH38A ·41H power reserve
CASE/DIAL	·Ø 40 mm ·316L Stainless steel case ·Sandwich dial with lumed bottom layer and cutouts to top layer ·Dial available in different colours
WATER RESISTANCE	100 m/10 atm
CRYSTAL	Sapphire crystal
LUME	Hands and indexes
STRAP	Leather or rubber
PRICE	395 £ (~458 €)

WHY BUY?

Despite this project is in the very first steps the watch looks really interesting specially for the deep rehaut that surrounds the dial,the playful colors and shape of the case. The price is totally in a good range for the features of the timepiece. Would be interersting in the future maybe see a steel bracelet option.

ENVISION
Prisma
AUTOMATIC
SWISS
MADE

Envision

Introducing a new watch brand onto the market involves the research for an identity character for the product. It all starts with the design and the shapes that will make real what was previously just an idea.

The founder of Envision, Alessandro, was driven by his passion for watchmaking to realise his own vision of the timepiece. After a scientific and legal education, he chose to follow his heart and immersed himself in this fascinating world, on a journey that started on a blank sheet of paper and evolved into the creation of something unique.
Three years of dedication, study, design and collaboration later, Prisma was out: a modern only-time watch with a rectangular case and integrated bracelet.

Envision is the first Italian independent brand that decided to introduce this watch shape, a rare feature outside the canons of luxury. The uniqueness of the design lies in its very unusual sapphire crystal, cut to create a prism effect that pleasantly distorts the view of the dial. The bracelet is perfectly integrated into the case, creating a sinuous and modern line.

This is just the beginning of Envision's ambitious project, a journey dedicated to research, beauty and emotion.

FOUNDER
Alessandro Bambini
•
FOUNDING YEAR
2023
•
COUNTRY
Italy
•
TYPE
Dress watch
•
MOVEMENT
Automatic
•
PRICE RANGE
1600 €
•
COLLECTIONS
1
•
WEBSITE
envision-watches.com

Prisma

MOVEMENT	· Automatic Swiss Sellita 200-1 · 38H power reserve
CASE/DIAL	· Ø 33 mm - 52 mm lug to lug · 316L stainless steel case · Soleil dial available in different colours · Applied indexes
WATER RESISTANCE	50 m/5 atm
CRYSTAL	Sapphire crystal
LUME	No
STRAP	Integrated stainless steel bracelet
PRICE	1600 €

Why buy?

The Prisma is featured by important dimensions, making this piece unsuitable for small wrists. However, the size ratio is correct and allows the complexity of the crystal design to be appreciated.

The price is justified by the design research and the quality of the materials, which are immediately noticeable, especially on the bracelet.

Fledermann
VON RIESTE
HANOVERIAN

Fledderman Von Rieste

The Fleddermann von Rieste story is one rooted deep in family pride and tradition. The founder comes from a strong German heritage, with roots in agriculture and metalworking. The desire to produce quality legacy timepieces is a labor of love and a passion for quality that provides a generational link.

Adam noticed the pride his father took in owning his grandfather's watch at a young age. He took note of the care his father gave it. Listening to the stories of family history, he felt the pride his great-grandfather must have had in his watch. Enamored by how his father cherished this watch, he learned that a timepiece was special. It was much more than a tool, it was a piece of pride. It has been cherished by each member of the Fledderman family who has owned it. Bought during the Great Depression, a sacrifice was made for the purchase. While this was not an ultra-luxury piece, it was still much more than a watch from the local discount store.

Witnessing the pride his father felt in owning his grandfather's watch never left Adam's soul. He remembered every moment of the first time he saw it, held it, hoped for it to be his one day. This memory stoked a fire to bring quality, dependable, and stylish timepieces to new customers.

FOUNDERS
Dr. Adam Fledderman

FOUNDING YEAR
2021

COUNTRY
USA

TYPE
Dress-Sports watch

MOVEMENT
Autoatic, hand wound

PRICE RANGE
599-1699 US$ (~566-1568 €)

COLLECTIONS
5

WEBSITE
vonrieste.com

THE HANOVERIAN

MOVEMENT	· Automatic Miyota 9015 · 42H power reserve
CASE/DIAL	· Ø 41 mm · 316L stainless steel angular case · Dial available in different colours · Embossed caseback
WATER RESISTANCE	150 m/15 atm
CRYSTAL	Sapphire crystal
LUME	Hands and indexes
STRAP	Stainless steel bracelet
PRICE	799 $ (~755 €)

THE MÜNCHNER

MOVEMENT	· Swiss hand-wound DB-6 series · 53H power reserve
CASE/DIAL	· Ø 44 mm · Polished 316L stainless steel case · Dial available in different colours · Small seconds hand · Embossed caseback
WATER RESISTANCE	50 m/5 atm
CRYSTAL	Sapphire crystal
LUME	Hands
STRAP	leather strap
PRICE	799 € (~755 €)

WHY BUY?

These watches are assembled in small batches by certified American Watchmaker and Clockmaker in Indiana and are realized with both modern and vintage soul.

As there are not many microbrands that are making watches with micro-second and manual winding movement, I think it's always interesting to discover something different.

The prices are honest for the products, just pay attention to the shipping and duty costs as the brand ships from USA.

GoS Watches

With a Master´s degree in Computer Science and Engineering and particular expertise in the medical field and computer security - Patrik has a sharp edge for minute details and an unshaken focus. Patrik trained at Swedish Watchmaking school, earning top honors. The Swedish watchmaking school is the only Scandanavian watchmaking school that is qualified for training and certification of watchmakers, on the level of a prestigious watchmaking school in Switzerland. Patrik has a highly developed ability to solve technical problems and his creativity and eye for details show in every GoS watch. He combines his theoretical knowledge and practical skills into preparing parts in damascus steel and finishing the parts. Patience is a requirement when a large number of steps have to be performed to reach the final results that highlight the details of the steel patterns.
Patrik follows the Swedish watchmaking tradition where watchmakers are not confined to work on the movement but all aspects of a watch: “The exterior is just as important to me as the interior of the watch.”

FOUNDER
Patrik Sjögren

•

FOUNDING YEAR
2007

•

COUNTRY
Sweden

TYPE
Dress watch

MOVEMENT
Automatic

PRICE RANGE
9500-42500 USD

COLLECTIONS
5+

•

WEBSITE
goswatches.com

Norrsken Fuchsia

MOVEMENT	·Automatic Gos customized from Schwartz Etienne ·86H power reserve
CASE/DIAL	·Ø 41.5 mm ·Stainless steel case ·Handcut northern-lights Guilloché with nano-ceramic based color
WATER RESISTANCE	50 m/5 atm
CRYSTAL	Sapphire crystal
LUME	Glass Index Ring
STRAP	Salmon Leather
PRICE	19500 $

Sarek Frost

MOVEMENT	·Automatic La Joux-Perret G101with anthrazite finish · 68H power reserve
CASE/DIAL	·Ø 41.5 mm ·Stainless steel case finishes inspired by viking bracelet ·Sunray finished dial in Ice blue or Midnight
WATER RESISTANCE	50 m/5 atm
CRYSTAL	Sapphire crystal
LUME	Indexes
STRAP	Premium Salmon leather with premium GoS pin-buckle
PRICE	9500 $

WHY BUY?

The finishes of all GoS watches are unbelievable, from the case to the bezel, the dial and the micro-rotor, every part of the watch is a work of art. There is a correct balance between highly polished and satin-finished surfaces. These watches are made with great craftsmanship and creativity and inspired by Sweden tradition and memories from the past. Pieces are limited and the price for the craftsmanship are very fair.

Hanhart
1882
FLYBACK
23 STEINE
Hanhart
1882
FLYBACK
23 STEINE

HANHART

Hanhart is today one of the best known and most historic independent watch companies. It all started in 1882 when Johann Adolf Hanhart opened his watch shop in Diessenhofen, Switzerland. He soon moved the business to Germany to enter a larger market, but it was his son Wilhelm who turned it into what it is today. His innovative vision was to start an affordable stopwatch manufacture that would be able to create tools designed by Hanhart himself for everyone. For the first time both an aesthetic and a functional concept would be applied to these gears. From idea to implementation, in 1924 the manufacture succeeded in bringing out its own first stopwatch. From this moment on, Hanhart started to produce more and more watches by expanding its model range.

Today, Hanhart is konwn worldwide for its pilot chronographs with their distinguishing red pusher. A functional idea born in 1938 to visually facilitate the pilot to push the right button which is still present in numerous models in the collection.
Actually, the brand's longevity lies precisely in its ability to adapt to the passage of time while maintaining its identity and connection to its roots.

The current catalogue is very rich and ranges from classic stopwatches to timepieces for motor sports, diving and aviation watches.

FOUNDER
Hanhart family

•

FOUNDING YEAR
1882

•

COUNTRY
Germany

•

TYPE
Pilot, stopwatch

•

MOVEMENT
Automatic
hand-wound

•

PRICE RANGE
850-2600 €

•

COLLECTIONS
5+

•

WEBSITE
hanhart.com

Pioneer Red X Blue

MOVEMENT	· Sellita AMT 5100 M · Small seconds · 58H power reserve
CASE/DIAL	· Ø 39 mm · 316L stainless steel case · Blue or navy · Fluted rotating bezel with red marking
WATER RESISTANCE	100 m/10 atm
CRYSTAL	Sapphire crystal
LUME	Hands and indexes
STRAP	Cowhide - suede finish
PRICE	2990 €

Primus Fly Navy

MOVEMENT	· Automatic Sellita SW510 · Small seconds · 42H power reserve
CASE/DIAL	· Ø 44 mm · 316L stainless steel case or black PVD · Navy blue dial · Chronocenter with "poseidon trident"
WATER RESISTANCE	100 m/10 atm
CRYSTAL	Sapphire crystal
LUME	Hands and indexes
STRAP	· Textil strap blue or black - Folding clasp steel/PVD
PRICE	3190 €

WHY BUY?

Although historic, Hanhart is to all intents and purposes an independent watchmaker that has managed to grow retaining its identity as a family business over the decades. Its production, which is small in comparison to the watchmaking giants, allows it to remain in the market segment that offers affordable yet high-quality watches in both workmanship and design.

Hanhart watches are an investment that transcends fashions thanks to the timeless appeal that encapsulates the memory of a tool that was revolutionary in its time. It is no coincidence that the models designed in the late 1930s are still part of the Hanhart collection: real gems that should not be missing from a collector's box.

MILUS
AUTOMATIC
WATER RESISTANT
300M / 1000FT
21

MILUS

Founded in 1919, Milus is a family-owned company, anchored in the heart of the Swiss watchmaking cradle, Biel.

Throughout its history, Milus was always seeking purity, elegance, flirting with the avant-garde, and always offering uncontestable price/quality/innovation ratio.

From luxurious to eminently refined, Milus watches have been at the forefront of the horological industry both in precision and technological innovation even winning multiple awards and being nominated for "The 50 brands of the Swiss watchmaking industry in the 20th century". The brand excels in creating timepieces that combine mechanical fineness and timeless design.

After three successive generations of craftsmanship, a new team, headed by the new CEO Luc Tissot, a descendant of the famous watch brand by the same name, is at the helm.

Today, the inspiration behind the core of the collection comes from Milus' own story. Through the collections, Snow Star, Archimèdes and LAB 01 Milus has reinterpreted important eras of the brand.

OWNER & CEO
Luc Tissot

•

FOUNDING YEAR
1919

•

COUNTRY
Switzerland

•

TYPE
Diver, dress watch

•

MOVEMENT
Automatic

•

PRICE RANGE
1090-2019 CHF
(~1100-2050 €)

•

COLLECTIONS
3

•

WEBSITE
milus.com

Archimèdes

MOVEMENT	·Swiss automatic ETA 2892A2 (TOP) ·42H power reserve
CASE/DIAL	·Ø 41 mm ·316L stainless steel case, brushed and polished finishing ·Bidirectional rotating internal bezel ·Dial available in different colours
WATER RESISTANCE	300 m/30 atm
CRYSTAL	Sapphire crystal
LUME	Hands, indexes, bezel
STRAP	Tropic dive rubber strap
PRICE	2019 CHF (~2050 €)

Snow Star

MOVEMENT	·Swiss automatic ETA 2892A2 (TOP) ·42H power reserve
CASE/DIAL	·Ø 39 mm ·Polished 904L Stainless steel case, open case back ·Sunray brushed dial available in different colours
WATER RESISTANCE	100 m/10 atm
CRYSTAL	Sapphire crystal
LUME	No
STRAP	904 Stainless steel bracelet
PRICE	1990 CHF (~1810 €)

LAB 01

MOVEMENT	• Swiss automatic Sellita SW200 • 38H power reserve
CASE/DIAL	• Ø 40 mm • 316L stainless steel case, polished and brushed finishing • Open caseback • Fiberglass dial available in different colours
WATER RESISTANCE	100 m/10 atm
CRYSTAL	Sapphire crystal both front and back
LUME	Hands and indexes
STRAP	Milanese mesh bracelet
PRICE	1090 CHF (~1100 €)

WHY BUY?

The wrist can immediately feel the quality of the materials, which has nothing to envy the most famous Swiss manufacturers despite the very competitive price. Smooth surfaces and a well-balanced size/weight ratio make Milus watches comfortable and elegant

The watch comes in simple yet sophisticated and up-to-date packaging: a useful and practical leather case containing separate watch and strap, as opposed to the usual cardboard boxes that are then abandoned.

50
55
60
NOSTAS
8

NOSTAS

The last few years have seen strong growth in the Italian watchmaking scene. There are many new brands that made their debut at Watches Of Italy, the Italian event dedicated to microbrands and independent brands. Among them, Nostas made the first debut at Vicenza Oro, another important italian jewels and watch fair and proved to be a young brand with a strong desire to make a name for itself and get noticed through their first collections AUDACE. Born from the creative mind of Francesco, founder and designer, and the support of his family, Nostas watches carry on the legacy of Italian 'know how': the perfect combination of timeless aesthetics and attention to detail.

The brand's language is expressed above all through the aggressive yet harmoniously balanced geometries of the octagonal case and bracelet.

The quest for perfection drives the production process, from conception to marketing; every detail is taken care of with the utmost attention, to create a final product of the highest standard. For this reason, Nostas only produces limited collections, which will never be reproduced again, thus enhancing the unique value of each individual watch.

FOUNDER
Francesco Nostas
•
FOUNDING YEAR
2019
•
COUNTRY
Italy
•
TYPE
Dress watch
•
MOVEMENT
Automatic
•
PRICE RANGE
610-850 €
•
COLLECTIONS
2
•
WEBSITE
nostasrome.com

AUDACE GMT

MOVEMENT	·Automatic Seiko NH34 ·41H power reserve
CASE/DIAL	·Ø 39 mm ·Polygonal 316L stainless steel case ·Bi-directional bezel 120 clicks available in different coloirs ·Blue or black pattern dial
WATER RESISTANCE	200 m/20 atm
CRYSTAL	Sapphire crystal
LUME	Hands and indexes
STRAP	·Stainless steel bracelet ·Quick release
PRICE	610 €

AUDACE

MOVEMENT	·Swiss automatic Sellita SW200 ·38H power reserve
CASE/DIAL	·Ø 39 mm ·Polygonal 316L stainless steel case ·Pattern dial available in different colours
WATER RESISTANCE	200 m/20 atm
CRYSTAL	Sapphire crystal
LUME	Hands and indexes
STRAP	·Stainless steel bracelet ·Quick release
PRICE	850 €

Audace 500

MOVEMENT	· Swiss automatic Sellita SW200 · 38H power reserve
CASE/DIAL	· Ø 41 mm · Polygonal 316L stainless steel case · Blue pattern dial
WATER RESISTANCE	500 m/50 atm
CRYSTAL	Sapphire crystal
LUME	Hands and indexes
STRAP	· Stainless steel bracelet and rubber strap · Quick release
PRICE	1200 €

Why buy?

This young brand still has a long way to go but the premises are certainly very good!

Despite their sharp shapes, Nostas watches are easy to wear with small dimensions to fit every wrist. The overall design is, in fact, very well balanced and highlights the detailed dial.
The colour combinations are sophisticated, I also particularly appreciate the version with rose gold details.

An extra point goes to the website: it is well designed and allows an excellent shopping experience for the user.

NSB
Canaveral
AUTOMATIC
200M/660FT
25
10
20
30
40
50

NSB WATCH

NSB Watch is a microbrand founded by the Italian interpreneur Matteo Micheletti. His passion comes from his grandfather and his childhood in Italy, close to the craftmanship tradition and the cult of beauty. However, it's the charm of Florida, his new home, that inspires NSB Watch collection. CANAVERAL rapresents the latest diver collection from NSB Watch and as Matteo says "The whole idea behind CANAVERAL was to capture true colors of the Canaveral National Seashore which is a protected area in Florida on the Cape." Depending on the colour of the timepiece there are 4 variants: SKY, SEASHORE, DRIFTWOOD, ISLAND. Each series represents an important feature of the Geographical area. The SEASHORE is characterized by a sand color for the dial to depict and remind about the miles and miles of pristine shores that Canaveral has, as well as the importance of keeping them untouched by man.The ISLAND Series has a pale mint green color for the dial and showcases the multitude of little islands dotted about the landscape around the Canaveral Preserve. DRIFTWOOD Series has a captivating dark brown dial representing the wet brown driftwood that is abundantly found in the marshes and waterways of Canaveral National Seashore. The Shuttle on the back is another symbol of Canaveral as it is famous for the Kennedy Space Center and what history it has attached with it for obvious reasons.

FOUNDER
Matteo Micheletti

FOUNDING YEAR
2018

COUNTRY
USA

TYPE
Diver, dress watch

MOVEMENT
Automatic

PRICE RANGE
100-750 US$ (~95-709 €)

COLLECTIONS
5+

WEBSITE
nsbwatch.com

Canaveral

MOVEMENT	• Automatic PT5000 or Swiss ETA 2824 • 42H power reserve
CASE/DIAL	• Ø 38 mm • 316L stainless steel case • Dial and bezel available in different colour combinations • Engraved caseback
WATER RESISTANCE	200 m/20 atm
CRYSTAL	Sapphire crystal
LUME	Bezel, hands, indexes
STRAP	Stainless steel bracelet
PRICE	397 US$ (~375 €)

Why buy?

This brand fully represents the Microbrand concept. In addition to the realisation of the watch itself also the possibility of representing what one is attached to, such as a place like the one the Canaveral series is representing.

The size of this watch makes it wearable for all types of wrists and the presence of the lume on the bezel as well as the possibility of choosing the movement make it even more interesting.

TACHYMETER
NUUN OFICIAL
NASA
CHRONOGRAPH
WATER RESISTANT
100m/328ft

NUUN OFFICIAL

Nuun Official takes its name from Halat Nuun, a small idyllic island off the southern coast of Bahrain.

Inspired by the legendary sports watches from the 1970s, Nuun timepieces deeply connect with the outdoors and adventures. They are made for people who want a time companion on the journey of life.

Never standing still, Nuun Official is always innovating and developing with new designs and materials that make them stand out as a brand. They blend the artisanship of contemporary watchmaking with the modern aesthetic and robustness, resulting in a timepiece that can handle anything. All while paying homage to the heritage of its remarkable birthplace, the Kingdom of Bahrain.

Up to now, this passion for adventure, experimentation and discovery has also brought great results on a social and community level.

Going in to 2024, Nuun Official plans a rebrand later this year, to strengthen market relationships and penetration. Currently in discussion with Swiss-based Fuzion agency, Nuun Official hopes to venture into Q4 with a water-tight strategy and sound future vision to tackle the 'affordable premium' category. It's clear that Nuun Official embrace innovation, not as a luxury, but as a standard.

FOUNDER
Talal Fakhro

FOUNDING YEAR
2017

COUNTRY
Bahrain

TYPE
Sport watch

MOVEMENT
Automatic, quartz

PRICE RANGE
159-2600 US$
(~148-2420 €)

COLLECTIONS
5+

WEBSITE
nuunofficial.com

N200 Gunmetal V2

MOVEMENT	·Seiko NH35A Automatic ·41H power reserve
CASE/DIAL	·Ø 40.5 mm ·Gunmetal 316L Sandblast Stainless steel case ·Display dial ·Arabic numbers
WATER RESISTANCE	200 m/20 atm
CRYSTAL	Sapphire crystal both front and back
LUME	Hands and indexes
STRAP	Caoutchouc rubber strap
PRICE	769 US$ (~706 €)

Origen N1837

MOVEMENT	·Quartz 1L40Miyota · 3 years power reserve
CASE/DIAL	·Ø 40.5 mm ·Sand blast finish dial available in different colours ·Carbon X tech case 316L PVD ·Steel case back ·Arabic numbers
WATER RESISTANCE	100 m/10 atm
CRYSTAL	K1 crystal
LUME	No
STRAP	Nanotech rubber strap
PRICE	395 US$ (~363 €)

MS SILVER

MOVEMENT	· Quartz GL20 Miyota · 5 years power reserve
CASE/DIAL	· Ø 38 mm · 316L stainless steel slim case brushed and polished · Guilloche dial available in different colors
WATER RESISTANCE	50 m/5 atm
CRYSTAL	Sapphire crystal
LUME	Hands
STRAP	Stainless steel bracelet or rubber strap
PRICE	495 USD (~454 €)

WHY BUY?

Each collection is related to a theme or a collaboration, approaching the watch concept more on an emotional than a material level: each model is a memory of an event, an experience or an action, so it is easy to find the one most akin to you.

Opting for a Nuun Official watch means choosing a brand that reimagines 'cool,' weaving each wearer's unique story into the fabric of its design.

OCEAN TO ORBIT
AUTOMATIC
LHOTSE
100m 330ft
SWISS MADE

Ocean To Orbit

Ocean To Orbit was founded in late 2020 by David and Siddhartha, two car designers with over 35 years of combined experience in the Auto industry.

Following a conversation about historical watches, centred on pieces worn by the great explorers and pioneers of the mid-20th century, during the expedition to Mount Everest, they decided to bring their experience and the process they learnt as designers to watch design with the purpose of creating their own everyday tool watch, the Lhotse.

The name is taken from the fourth highest mountain in the world at 8516m, and means south peak in Tibetan, where the watch was also worn and tested by Nepali mountaineer and photojournalist Purnima Shrestha on her expedition in May 2022.

So, this watch is not just an elegant piece of design, it's also a purpose-built tool watch engineered to perform in the harshest of conditions. In addition to this the Lhotse is the first collection created by the brand and will be available in four core variants, plus a limited edition dedicated to their local watch community, Watch Enthusiasts Melbourne.

FOUNDERS
David Dewitt & Siddhartha Kazami
FOUNDING YEAR
2020
•
COUNTRY
Australia
•
TYPE
Sport watch
•
MOVEMENT
Automatic
•
PRICE RANGE
925-975 USD$ (~860-907 €)
•
COLLECTIONS
1
•
WEBSITE
oceantoorbit.com

Lhotse

MOVEMENT	·Swiss automatic STP 1-21 ·40H power reserve
CASE/DIAL	·Ø 38.5 mm ·316L Stainless Steel Case ·Engraved Caseback ·Dial available in different colors
WATER RESISTANCE	100 m/10 atm
CRYSTAL	Sapphire crystal with A/R
LUME	Hands and indices
STRAP	Stainless Steel Bracelet
PRICE	925-975USD$

Why buy?

The Lhotse is characterized by its sculptural design and refined finishes. Clearly inspired by some well known timepieces from the major brands, this watch features a beautifully finished dial with a vertically brushed surface, applied indices and logo, powerful BGW9 superluminova and a box dome sapphire crystal with colorless AR coating. The hands, also unique to this watch, are inspired by the brands name and feature a rocket ship hour hand. At 38.5mm in diameter and 47mm lug to lug, this watch is expressive, stylish, and sophisticated.

OPHION

OPHION

The Ophion brand is certainly among the independent brands that have received a lot of interest, especially in recent years. First of all, we are talking about a Spanish brand and this makes us realise how interesting brands can be found in different locations.

The goal of the brand is very clear, offering the experience of the high end watches but and a much affordable level, this because usually is very difficult to find the characteristics of the Haute Horology in affordable pieces. The name of the brand Ophion, comes from Greek Mythology, Ophion was the first Titan he and his wife created the universe, and were the parents of all the gods, including Cronos, known for being the god of time. They liked the idea of Ophion being the father of the god of time and that's why they choose this name.

Almost everything in their watches is curved, domed or round. This has been a difficult challenge when producing all the components because usually surfaces are flat and straight, that make them easier to be produced. They break the industry standards in the name of a refined design.

FOUNDER
Miguel Morales Ribas

FOUNDING YEAR
2014

COUNTRY
Spain

TYPE
Dress watch

MOVEMENT
Hand wound

PRICE RANGE
3420-15000 €

COLLECTIONS
4

WEBSITE
ophion-watches.com

OPH 411 Vesper

MOVEMENT	· Custom hand wound Schwarz Etienne · 86H power reserve
CASE/DIAL	· Ø 39 mm · Hand polished 316L stainless steel case · Multilayered dial with laser-cut micro indexes available in different colours · Nickel plated hands
WATER RESISTANCE	50 m/5 atm
CRYSTAL	Sapphire crystal both front and back with anti-reflect coating
LUME	Hands
STRAP	Hand made leather strap
PRICE	7950 €

VELOS

MOVEMENT	· Hand-wound custom movement produced in collaboration with MHVJ and Soprod · 120H power reserve
CASE/DIAL	· Ø 39 mm · Hand-polished 316L stainless steel case · Multi-layerd dial available in different colours and pattern
WATER RESISTANCE	50 m/5 atm
CRYSTAL	Sapphire crystal
LUME	No
STRAP	Leather strap
PRICE	3620 €

WHY BUY?

This brand is yet another example of how one can have a high level watch at a price that is truly accessible to all. The open back always allows us to observe the beauty of the movements which, although not manufactured, are modified according to the brand's specifications to make them even more interesting.

The dials and the lines and finish of the case are of the highest quality. The brand makes very limited editions. At the moment, I think it is as a quality/price ratio an excellent choice.

SHERWOOD
AUTOMATIC
BRITISH
DESIGN

Sherwood Watches

Could a watch inspired by the historic Sherwood Forest inspire buyers to part with their cash? The answer is yes! Glynn Reynolds, a watch designer from Mansfield — just a short arrows shot away from the fabled home of the outlaw Robin Hood — has crafted a truly breathtaking piece. Proof that microbrands can draw inspiration from their immediate surroundings, be it towns, cities, or in this case Sherwood Forest.

Glynn's croudfunding campaign has certainly hit the bullseye with over £30,000 raised to manufacture the watch.

About the watch itself, it's called the Commander and available in three colours, green, blue and black. The most attractive model is the green one, inspired by the hues of Sherwood Forest. Both the colour of the dial and the bezel are a striking green.

The watch features a 40mm case with applied indexes and a strong presence of lumen on both the indexes, hands and the bezel. The subtle reference to Robin Hood illustrated by the seconds hand entirely arrow-shaped will make great macro photos for your social photos!

FOUNDER
Glynn Reynolds

FOUNDING YEAR
2023

COUNTRY
UK

TYPE
Diver Watch

MOVEMENT
Automatic

PRICE RANGE
450£ (520€)

COLLECTIONS
1

WEBSITE
sherwoodwatches.com

COMMANDER - GREEN

MOVEMENT	· Automatic Miyota 9039 · 42 power reserve
CASE/DIAL	· Ø 40 mm · 316L stainless steel case · Sunburst Dial available in different colours · BG W9 Lume (green dial has C3 lume)
WATER RESISTANCE	200 m/20 atm
CRYSTAL	Sapphire crystal
LUME	Hands, indexes, bezel
STRAP	Stainless steel bracelet
PRICE	450£ (520€)

WHY BUY?

The reference to Robin Hood is clever but not the only attraction to this gorgeous timepiece. The price of 450 pounds is bang on the money for a 200 meter diver watch.

The attention to detail is astonishing. A ceramic bezel and premium miyota 9039 movement is classy and the contrast between polished and brushed finishes on the case and the bracelet is another thoughtful touch.

Not bad for a first collection!

HIDAKA SHINICHI

SHINICHI HIDAKA

Shinichi Hidaka is a young watchmaker based in Tokyo.

After graduating from high school, he couldn't find a personal direction, so he spent time without a clear purpose for a period.

After discovering a series of watchmaking animations and videos on the Internet, Shinichi became very passionate of the world of self-learning watchmaking.
In 2022 he started studying and experimenting this art with the purpose of creating his own watch brand.

His timepieces are playful and elegant at the same time. Passion has been translated into the creation of five collections in a very short time. Each model is made by Shinichi himself in limited quantities.

One of his most succesful timepieces realized is the IZANAGI, a dress watch featured by an aventurine dial that evokes a starry sky.

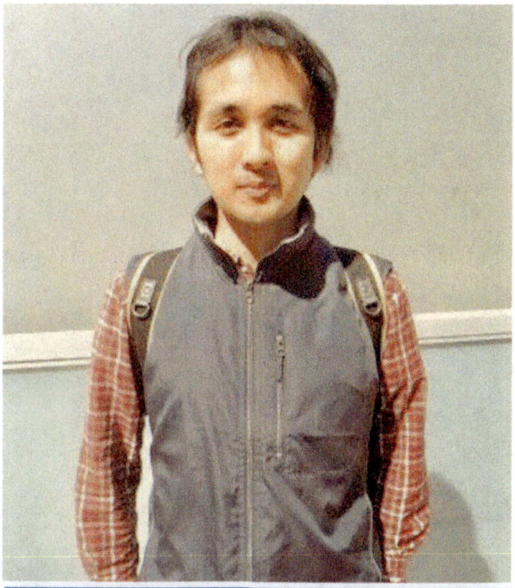

FOUNDER
Shinichi Hidaka
•
FOUNDING YEAR
2022
•
COUNTRY
Japan
•
TYPE
Dress watch
•
MOVEMENT
Automatic, Hand wound
•
PRICE RANGE
1000-5000 US$
(~980-4900 €)
•
COLLECTIONS
5
•
WEBSITE
shinichi-watch.myshopify.com

Shimadzu

MOVEMENT	· Hand wound Unitas 6498 4/3 Plate Swan Neck · 42H power reserve
CASE/DIAL	· Ø 41 mm · 316L Stainless Steel · Small Seconds · Baked blue steel leaf hands
WATER RESISTANCE	50 m/5 atm
CRYSTAL	Sapphire crystal
LUME	No
STRAP	Leather strap
PRICE	1900 US$ (~1680€)

Arakawa Sector Dial

MOVEMENT	· Automatic Sellita SW200 · 38H power reserve
CASE/DIAL	· Ø 36 mm · Case 316L · Sector dial · Leaf hands Burnished blue hands Silver hands
WATER RESISTANCE	50 m/5 atm
CRYSTAL	Sapphire crystal
LUME	No
STRAP	Leather strap
PRICE	990 US$ (~840 €)

WHY BUY?

The beauty of these watches is in the appeal of Japanese culture and the use of different materials such as aventurine, also used by very important brands.

Obviously we are talking about a young watchmaker who is just starting out and therefore needs to be given time to evolve, but the premises are absolutely excellent.

STEFANO BRAGA
WATCHES
HUGINN
100 MT - 330 FEET
SWISS MADE

Stefano Braga Watches

Stefano Braga is a Swiss brand focused on both quartz and automatic watches with very competitive features. The current collection consists of three main models, Huginn for the automatic collection, Prometheus and Athmos for the quartz collection.

Huginn is a raven in Norse mythology, associated with the god Odin. Huginn and his 'brother' Muninn represent not only Odin's ravens, but also the concept of duality. Huginn it means "thought" and indeed the watch is very solid and robust. With this model, Stefano Braga wanted to launch his thought, inspired by aviator — pilot watches combined with a refined design.

Prometheus was the first Titan to steal the sacred fire of the gods (metaphorically recognised as Knowledge) and give it to mankind as a gift. He can be seen as a symbol of rebellion and defiance of the authorities, since is gesture in favour of humanity was severely punished by the king of the gods. This watch represents all this: knowledge (complete calendar), rebellion (design) with an attractive and versatile profile.

"Athmos" comes from "athmosphere", as a tribute to the beauty of the world. The indexes represent the four cardinal points and the small seconds counter evokes the power of wind through its "vortex" design.

FOUNDER
Stefano Braga
•
FOUNDING YEAR
2020
•
COUNTRY
Switzerland
•
TYPE
Dress watch
•
MOVEMENT
Automatic, quartz
•
PRICE RANGE
415-3700 CHF (~440-3900€)
•
COLLECTIONS
5+
•
WEBSITE
stefanobragawatches.com

Huginn

MOVEMENT	·Swiss automatic SBW110 modified from Catena SA110 ·40H power reserve
CASE/DIAL	·Ø 40 mm ·316L stainless steel case with engraved caseback ·Textured dial available in different colours
WATER RESISTANCE	100 m/10 atm
CRYSTAL	Sapphire crystal
LUME	Hands and indexes
STRAP	·Italian hand-made vegetable leather ·Quick release
PRICE	990 CHF (~1070 €)

Prometheus

MOVEMENT	·Quartz Swiss R.706.3 ·60 months power reserve
CASE/DIAL	·Ø 40 mm ·316L stainless steel case or DLC ·Perpetual calendar ·Pattern dial available in different colours ·Applied indexes
WATER RESISTANCE	100 m/10 atm
CRYSTAL	Sapphire crystal
LUME	Hands and indexes
STRAP	Black silicon strap
PRICE	460-490 CHF (~530 €)

WHY BUY?

Despite quartz watches are little considered, Stefano Braga has managed to make this type of watch interesting as well by integrating a complete calendar and a very special dial.

Concerning the automatic, it is very comfortable on the wrist thanks to the well proportionate dimensions.

Another important good point is the focus of sustainability with recycled box and vegetal leather.

STREHLER

Strehler Watches

Andreas Strehler is an independent watchmaker well known for making handmade timepieces with totally in-house movements of the highest standard with incredible complications.

Among his most famous movements and watches we can mention the Sauterelle a Lune Perpetuelle characterized by hour, minute, small second, constant force, phase of the moon indication with a deviation of one day in 2 million years! Another important timepiece by Andreas Strehler is the Papillon d'or, which features a butterfly-shaped bridge, from *papillon* , the name of the butterfly in French.

As can be guessed, the watches made by Andreas are not affordable for everyone, characterised by very high prices. Despite this, Mr. Strehler decided to use his incredible expertise to create a new watch called SIRNA — not cheap but at reasonable price for the materials used and craftmaship — under a new name, Strehler.

This new brand focuses on making watches with the same DNA as Andreas Strehler's timepieces. The goal is not to propose personalized creation, but rather a more widely attainable daily piece that still have the Andreas Strehler design and engineering inside.

FOUNDER
Andreas Strehler
•
FOUNDING YEAR
2023
•
COUNTRY
Switzerland
•
TYPE
Dress watch
•
MOVEMENT
Automatic
•
PRICE RANGE
20000 CHF (~21000 €)
•
COLLECTIONS
1
•
WEBSITE
strehler.watch

Sirna

MOVEMENT	· Automatica SA-30 · 60H power reserve · 18k gold rotor
CASE/DIAL	· Ø 40 mm · Medical-grade stainless steel case · Titanium dial, laser engraved, hand polished, anodised in blue with proprietary pattern · Circular-brushed ss chapter ring
WATER RESISTANCE	30 m/3 atm
CRYSTAL	Sapphire crystal front and back
LUME	No
STRAP	· Calf leather strap · Quick release
PRICE	20000 CHF (~21000 €)

WHY BUY?

Independent watchmaking is well known for its high prices that are unattainable for most people on earth and especially for watches that are not really wearable every day, which is why they are considered collector's items, to be placed in the shop window and observed every now and then, a bit like a work of art.

Strehler, on the other hand, aims to make this 'art' wearable every day and at a figure that is certainly affordable if we consider the average prices of independent watchmaking and only affordable by collectors with multi-million dollar fortunes. SIRNA presents itself with a diameter suitable for all wrists, materials of the highest quality such as titanium for the dial with its unique pattern or the medical steel. From the open back it is possible to appreciate the 18k gold rotor and the various technique of finishing on movement in its entirety.

ROMANO ALBERTI
ITALY
Ō-YOROI

TIME CHANGERS

TimeChangers aims to reinterpret the past to create watches rich in personality and quality. Each watch, made in a limited and numbered series, has its own story to tell and is the fruit of years of research and the savoir-faire of Italian master craftsmen.

The source of inspiration is Italian art, the undisputed pride of the *Bel Paese*, and the millenary cultures beyond its borders, starting with Japan.

To date, there are two collections proposed by this company: O-YOROI, a tribute to the legendary figure of the Samurai, and NAKED BIKE, inspired by the Italian motorbikes that have made history in the world of racing.

O-YOROI, a collection rich in symbolism, is a tribute by designer Romano Alberti to the legendary figure of the Samurai, warrior of ancient Japan, and his philosophy of life. The watch, a true *objet d'art*, wishes to evoke a "duel" between two *bushi* in constant study and observation, heedless of the inexorable passage of time. The dial and crown are reminiscent of head protection (*Kabuto*), the crown guard is reminiscent of shoulder protection (*Sode*), while the distinctive elements of arm protection (*Kote*), torso protection (*Do*), belly protection (*Kusazuri*), leg protection (*Haidate*) and foot protection (*Sune-ate*) are found around the case and in the lugs.

TIME CHANGERS
ITALY

FOUNDERS
Roberto Janniello, Fausto Lancini, Romano Alberti

FOUNDING YEAR
2014

COUNTRY
Italy

TYPE
Dress watch, chronograph

MOVEMENT
Automatic, quartz

PRICE RANGE
999-8800 €

COLLECTIONS
2

WEBSITE
timechangers.it

O-YOROI

MOVEMENT	·Swiss automatic Sellita SW260-1 ·38H power reserve
CASE/DIAL	·Ø 43 mm ·316L stainless steel case ·Stainless bezel with black resin ·Display case back
WATER RESISTANCE	30 m/3 atm
CRYSTAL	Sapphire crystal both front and back
LUME	Hands and indexes
STRAP	Leather strap
PRICE	8800 €

NAKED BIKE

MOVEMENT	·Quartz Miyota 6S11 · 4 years power reserve
CASE/DIAL	·Ø 48 mm ·Titaniun case with custom tubolar frame ·Titanium screwed case back ·Multi-level colored dial
WATER RESISTANCE	30 m/3 atm
CRYSTAL	Mineral crystal
LUME	Hands
STRAP	Leather strap
PRICE	999 €

Why buy?

Choose O-Yoroi if you want to wear a unique timepiece, a true piece of art rich in symbolism and drawing its inspiration from millenary Japanese culture. It is delivered in a precious wooden box hand-painted in Italy.

Choose Naked Bike if you want to wear a watch that draws heavily from the construction technique typical of motorbikes that have made history in the racing world. Naked Bike comes in an aluminum case.

BASE 30 PULSATIONS
VERIWATCH
20 ATMOS
AUTOMATIC
SWISS
MADE

VeriWatch

In 1956, in a workshop in the heart of Bari, an Apulian city overlooking the Adriatic Sea, the watch brand VeriWatch was born.

In 2023, thanks to the resourcefulness of the Brescian entrepreneur Alessandro Leali, the brand is back in the limelight with a new revised version of the Octopus, the Bari-based brand's flagship watch that contributed to making medical diver history. Its main feature is confirmed to be the pulsometer scale on a 30 base that, displayed on the inner flange, serves to determine the heart rate expressed in beats per minute.

Designed in Italy and made in Switzerland, the new VeriWatch Octopus, water-resistant to 200 meters, features the characteristic case of the Skin Diver watches of the 1960s and 1970s, a golden age for diver's watches, while the caseback offers, as a novelty, a relief embossed reproducing the "ringed" tentacles typical of octopuses. The VeriWatch Octopus comes with three customised straps: a Tropical Legend, a Tropical Sport and a soft NATO strap in 100% recycled polyester with 316L steel loops and buckle.

VERIWATCH
SINCE1956

FOUNDER
Alessandro Leali

FOUNDING YEAR
2023

COUNTRY
Italy

TYPE
Diver

MOVEMENT
Automatic

PRICE RANGE
1050 €

COLLECTIONS
1

WEBSITE
veriwatch.it

Octopus 1973

MOVEMENT	·Swiss automatic Sellita SW200-1A ·38H power reserve
CASE/DIAL	·Ø 38 mm ·316L stainless steel case ·120 click stainless steel bezel ·Pulsometer scale ·Embossed caseback
WATER RESISTANCE	200 m/20 atm
CRYSTAL	Sapphire crystal
LUME	Hands and indexes
STRAP	Rubber or NATO strap
PRICE	1050 €

WHY BUY?

Reviving a watch brand and relaunching it is not easy. Today, the market really offers many types of diver and the competition is really high. In spite of this, VeriWatch manages to distinguish itself with characteristics and quality of materials that are certainly interesting and on a par with many brands that have been active for even longer. Strong points are the bezel, the pulsometric scale and the decoration on the back.

VITREUM
VITRØS EMAILLE

VITREUM

Vitreum is an independent watch brand renowned for its dedication to crafting high-end mechanical watches adorned with traditional grand feu enamel dials. At Vitreum, the creation of each timepiece is a meticulous process that combines patience, years of experience, and unparalleled skill.

It all begins with the intricate hand-engraving of sterling silver dials, a labour-intensive task that sets the foundation for the mesmerising beauty to come. Layers of enamel glass are delicately applied to the engraved surface, meticulously built up and heated in a kiln to achieve a flawless, glass-like finish. Since debuting the Rare Handcrafts collection in 2022, Vitreum has continued to captivate watch enthusiasts with a series of mesmerising pieces of art, including the Storm & Sea, five unique freehand engraved enamel pieces inspired by Edo Period Japanese art and Welsh nature and Ammonite, champlevé enamel inspired by the intricate beauty of an ancient ammonite fossil. This year marks a significant milestone for Vitreum as they proudly unveil their inaugural entry in the long-awaited Core Collection: Arctic Blue, with a dial bathed in deep blue enamel and a hand-engraved texture reminiscent of serene landscapes frozen in time.

VITREUM

FOUNDERS
Kasper Reisner
& Naomi Nevill

FOUNDING YEAR
2018

COUNTRY
Denmark - UK

TYPE
Dress watch

MOVEMENT
Hand wound

PRICE RANGE
2495-4495 €

COLLECTIONS
2

WEBSITE
vitreumwatches.com

FH01 Arctic Blue - Core Collection

MOVEMENT	· Swiss hand-wound Sellita SW210 · 42H power reserve
CASE/DIAL	· Ø 39.5 mm · 316L stainless steel case · Hand-engraved sterling silver with deep blue enamel · Arabic numerals inspired by 14th century writing
WATER RESISTANCE	50 m/5 atm
CRYSTAL	Sapphire crystal
LUME	No
STRAP	Handmade Nubuck leather strap
PRICE	2495 €

FH01 Storm & Sea - Rare Handcrafts

MOVEMENT	· Swiss hand-wound Sellita SW210 · 42H power reserve
CASE/DIAL	· Ø 39.5 mm · 316L Stainless s. Freehand-engraved motif inspired by Welsh nature and Edo-Period Japanese art
WATER RESISTANCE	50 m/5 atm
CRYSTAL	Sapphire crystal
LUME	No
STRAP	Handmade Nubuck leather strap
PRICE	4495 €

WHY BUY?

Vitreum is committed to preserving the captivating art of grand feu enamel through its unique watch designs. Every dial is meticulously hand-crafted by skilled enamelers in one of Vitreum's workshops in Denmark and Wales. Their watches represent the intersection of tradition and innovation, embodying the essence of classic craftsmanship fused with modern design aesthetics.

Photo Credits

P.14 Apiar watches: @Realwatchbrothers ; P.28 Bauche Watches: @eddiesng1011

All the pictures not mentioned above are courtesy of their respective brands.

Contributors

Project leader: Giuseppe Marasco
Graphics: Virginia Barbieri
Text editing: Silvia Operato

Printed in Dunstable, United Kingdom

82308733R00078